Destructive Heresies

Destructive Heresies
© Miloh E. Gorgevska / Cathexis Northwest Press

No part of this book may be reproduced without written permission of the publisher or author, except in reviews and articles.

First Printing: 2022

Paperback ISBN: 978-1-952869-67-9

Cover & Interior by C. M. Tollefson
Editing by C. M. Tollefson & Airea Johnson

Cathexis Northwest Press

cathexisnorthwestpress.com

Destructive Heresies

Poetry by Miloh E. Gorgevska

Cathexis Northwest Press

To all those who have loved,
and have only ever tried to love.

Thank you to my editor, Courtney Bambrick. I gained a sense of pride in my work because of your faith in it, and you helped me polish it until I was confident in it. Thank you to the editors of *Thi Wurd* for publishing "Lilith's Love Letter to Eve" and *Near Window* for publishing "Firmly Planted By Streams Of Water" and "As I Have Loved You." And thank you to the editors of *Wingless Dreamer* for publishing "According to Your Abundant Mercy," albeit under a different name and read.

Table of Contents

SUMMER

To Eat Its Fruit	23
Entrust My Life	24
Precious & Honoured	26
Lilith's Love Letter To Eve	27
According to Your Abundant Mercy	28

AUTUMN

Bind Them Around Your Heart	33
Firmly Planted By Streams Of Water	34
Lightning From Heaven	35
Salvation in No One Else	36
As I Have Loved You	37

WINTER

Utterly Scorned	41
Wages of Sin	42
& Now These Three Remain	44
Hallowed Be Your Name	50
West of Eden	51
Outside in the Streets & Inside in the Safest Room	52

Spring

Sacred Stones	57
Wealth Without Knowing	58
To The Glory	59
The Power of The Tongue	60

SUMMER

Psalm 32:4
For day and night your hand was heavy on me; my strength was sapped as in the heat of summer.

To Eat Its Fruit

1.
april strikes
i pray for change
a light in darkness

[light appears]

fire in the night
this house could talk
but me—
i lose my memory

2.
vengeance for the sake
of a woman with
too many husbands

summer always comes too soon

now things
are where they are & will end
where they're destined
to end

Entrust My Life

the balkan sun welcomed me to you
                            strangers to each other in the dead heat
                                & yet you became my healer

***

oddly met, with back against the world
unaware of who i would blossom to be
                            thorny rose awed by your own stickability

***

the way we are
            is the way we are
                & i wouldn't wish for it any other way

joy like nobody else's

people packed it up nice before   wrapped with finest papers

                        & tied in red, but only you knew i love yellow

tell me about the trees or how it was raining all day
                          & you, stuck inside were cool
                          'coz at least you talked to me

***

neat how we can be so different
            yet still on the same page
                        watching the same movie

& you know i love those action films   all the same tropes:
staying alive in a situation where   the guy
                      against all odds

to confront hostility without fear   /   selflessly sacrifice
    himself to save others   /   rescue the woman he loves
            but you're guaranteed explosions

                        & in that world everything works how it should
                    & it's okay that in this world it doesn't because
                we're all bound by the desire it would

***

isn't it true & good
    that we all try to make it so
day by day

        the way you say my name   reminds me that the yellows
        of the world make up   for all the stuff
                we've had to live through

***

you say the sun will always rise
      & paint the world resplendent
    you who will pack that joy for me & you who will deliver it to me

***

but an excess of baggage will cause agoraphobia &
        enough misanthropy to cause you to miss your flight
           & never even take off
           in the first place

Precious & Honoured

isn't it enough to wish for what we already have
here in the rings of our tree trunk

to still feel you, places where words won't reach—
touch alone

carrying fear & fear still feels lighter near you
endless stream of this & that & this

perhaps your leaving will be a hurricane
the waves will leave nothing that doesn't belong

but when we return the fire will burn
& twist to fit our new lives

but always burning & burning & every corner i've turned away
leads to the same path: it is enough, you say

it is enough
to be where we are

Lilith's Love Letter To Eve

can you say this world is better? or
would you, with your eyes closed?
are we still holy?

have these wings seen their last clouds?
have our constellations finally
been swallowed by novas?

one night with these fine tastes
you, ethereal & i, electric
energy that bites in the right ways

just outside of town our crumbling home
with the vines green on green
eating & climbing the walls

a river to swim in—O, how it surrounds us!
crystal blue & yearning moss smelling like
sweat & the sun's beams shining through a whiskey bottle

a blanket we've woven underneath our skin
mango juice dripping down our chins
the fruit so intoxicating & may you be the apple

when i say i'm dreaming
i mean, i wish God let
dreams come true

According to Your Abundant Mercy

plant died on my balcony some six months ago now

    reminders list will beep each Thursday
        begging me to get my shit together & sit up straighter

        a grating diapason stuck on a loop spinning like gales of grief
            around & around & around

            my first home engulfed in the tempest
                —purposes & purposes lost

                can't say i know where you're meant to carry
                    the phantom of a dead thing—small & unescorted

            every corner of this heavenly body seems different now
                sacred rays riddling & riddling & riddling

            inevitability of all naked dreams leaving us only with august:
                forge & harbinger of things going to sleep for good

where there is no good
    where the only good is

                                        i'll move it tomorrow

AUTUMN

Jude 1:12
These people are blemishes at your love feasts, eating with you without the slightest qualm—shepherds who feed only themselves. They are clouds without rain, blown along by the wind; autumn trees, without fruit and uprooted—twice dead.

Bind Them Around Your Heart

there's an art to each leaf's veins that longs
to be discovered, almost like a puzzle

& leaves sing to each other in the wind as they fall
like how your laughter seems to echo mine

well maybe i am not the kind of person who can
dance in moonlight & dig heels into dirt

hold hands for long & for longer still
maybe my edges are sharp enough to cut

couldn't say if that's what you've been looking for
couldn't promise my love would be undying

or even worth-the-while
but in our veins lay a delicate pattern

like the ice that makes up snowflakes—
the fun kind, that packs & sticks together

synchronicity of things aligning
falling debris becoming a catalyst

unlike any other & so unwise
to explore & yet an unopened mystery

sorry for ignoring all the ways it will
melt one day & sorry, sorry for fantasizing about

how we could fit so well together

Firmly Planted By Streams Of Water

you see what you want in the surface of trees
at false spring i looked & a face was staring back at me

trees talk if you listen closely to their swaying, their roots reach out
connected by fungi & speak like us & mourn their deaths
maybe you believe me when i tell you i have faith
in the astrological compatibility of trees

& instead of running late, we arrive, but i've long since
learned that this life's story never ends as we imagine

so i'll invent some other world
where i look & it's you

looking back at me

Lightning From Heaven

i see you rotting in my dreams
                         face dripping straight down

what i would have done & how i changed the shape of my soul
& where i sheared my body to fit you proper & ladylike

when i loved first i believed in four leaf clovers
do i love you still if i keep them pressed in my journal?

my life as a self-flagellation, never once forgetting
& scarcely forgiving the choices i've made

i remember the people i've hurt
more than people who've hurt me

& i know, you cannot control how others will paint you
only the resemblance to the source image

& yet, drawn the same way so many times i grow attached
to this version where i am a subject no image can capture kindly

&
can i live without needing to control?

death of all i ever yearned for & secrets i whisper in the dark
ones that say i would rather starve than be fulfilled &

would rather live in a world where each line i say
has been carefully rehearsed in a mirror

Salvation in No One Else

without fanfare or notice, you changed the locks on me
& i started knocking until my knuckles were bleeding

it is a strange death & a starvation of epiphany
focused only on your forgotten memory

must i delete every inch of you & trace the markers in my DNA
find the parts you've imprinted in & sever them from my body?

i am not sure why i cannot leave
i am not sure whether i have baggage left inside

my final pack of cigarettes sitting on your kitchen counter?
the seasons i have spent dreaming of your living room?

when you first welcomed me in, everything was warm
but it's mid-March now & i am stuck outside

evicted, my feet
have frozen in my shoes

As I Have Loved You

slowly we wake
time & again, absence blocks day
& when it finally arrives

                                        the light isn't what you imagined
                                        it would look like

we won't know any more by nightfall
but ashes & ashes will surround us just until
the morning comes, or so our heaviness hopes

                                        where do ghosts go
                                        when they're through?

do they follow someone else around
darker than a cloudy shadow?
is all we carry all we've ever carried

                                        in circles & circles
                                        & circles?

when you go it will feel like ice
my fingertips will burn against the frigid air
wishing i was anywhere else

                                        but the sun that bleeds us
                                        is holy & unforgiving

on the threshold of where we met, i sit with my legs crossed
& dream of a world where i am well enough to love you well
are you as sorry as i am? sniveling & sobbed out

                                        nothing ever enough
                                        to last or feed me?

sacred hollow mind longing for something like peace
if i write this quietly enough maybe no one will notice

when we're gone

WINTER

1 Corinthians 16:6
Perhaps I will stay with you for a while, or even spend the winter, so that you can help me on my journey, wherever I go.

Utterly Scorned

isn't it strange
the people we cling to in our darkest days

a cimmerian shine   on nights where   there is no sorrow

but   only
                        emptiness &   the   strange   feeling
you've   forgotten something   or left it   behind

love   in all its faces   spent on the wrong   dice
          young & openhearted
              forced into a den of lions   we ache for something greater

in a life whose only purpose   is to survive—
it's strange

              how you've   held   onto your kindness

throughout every wringing

     how you've held all your blood

                   in spite of every leech

                         who's fooled you into feeling

                                            loved

Wages of Sin

    years later & i find i don't have the patience
to love somebody new anymore.

        years & years later — i can see it now— i am crying over the loss of You

i was falling forward & i screamed *Catch me, Catch me*
      i wanted so badly for you to be the one who caught me
Catch me, Catch me:
       & i watched the light leave
                                  Your eyes

i was always afraid of you dying
didn't really realize death could look like this, too

                                              this:
             light leaves   /   eyes roll back   /   or maybe glaze over
                    doesn't really change   anything

                              this:
           blood replaced   with hardening cement   sinking deeper into
                            the ground

                this:
            exhale   /   inhale   /   breath never leaves
                doesn't really change   anything

in my dreams You're there   & i am fixing all my wrongs
making the cocktail so perfect   You won't choke   You'll drink & finish
brilliant & happily   in love   with me

                      You wouldn't catch me

    & when i wake i am always falling somewhere through the atmosphere
            deeper into the earth beyond even where
        You
           are buried

i didn't realize death could look like
                       this

i didn't realize i could make you a part me of
      only for   You   to sever yourself
                      from my body

it was so quiet when you died

i didn't realize death could look like someone alive
                someone breathing in the flesh
                  but still gone & still gone from me

i still text you sometimes
even though

& Now These Three Remain

12:03am
hey, im sorry to bother you

it's just

i can feel my pulse in every part of my body
racing & raging through me

& really i don't want to upset you

but im afraid of what will happen
next

2:47am
hey, it's me again

i know you said i should stop calling but

i can't stop thinking about
that time i got really high in your car

it's funny now thinking i barely knew you
& yet you stayed with me til i came
down

i thought i would die

not you too

4:23am
ok, so it's me again

i know you haven't blocked my number
because my messages keep going through

so i won't repeat myself
because i can see our history
laid out just above me

where i pour my heart out to you
& you never even open

but you still let me speak

so i'll keep talking

til i finally talk myself
out of it

Hallowed Be Your Name

i prayed empty phrases   at your altar   & you became my king
seeking   your salvation   dignified & sober minded   i was ever faithful
putting   coals   in   my mouth
there is no devotion   here   look away   look somewhere else
i am willing to pray no longer
i am willing to trade prayers for silence   my fool's voice   with many words

i am willing to hold onto nothing   anymore chased away   like a vision

     i stripped naked for you   i i stripped to my bones   for you

that you may do no wrong   that that that you may do what   is right

     begging: i am all out   of pray pray prayer   went searching in your

eyes   green yet barren   warm for babies animals & old friends

cold as you say   i love you   c cold as you say   i want to be with

you   c co cold as you say   i understand you   anyway this isn't

about you   this is about prayer   it's lost from me   thrown into the

outer darkness   i made a practice of sinning   i i i stripped bare   i

stripped bare for you   anyway this isn't about you   i am trying to find

a prayer   f f f forgive me   my trespasses   i am trying to find

myself & the strength   the will   my parting will   the will

will my eulogy   have any poetry   will my epitaph say   they

were loved   when i die i hope i die in your embrace   but this isn't about

you   this is about   breath   breathing & i   can no longer

breathe   can no longer sing   sing sing singing   but you aren't

listening   anyway   a a a anyway   this isn't   about you.

West of Eden

a thousand times i've lived this story
the ending & answers in plain

starving filled my eyes, he said
never saw his own reflection / his own hunger

& i'd only ever break those eggshells he hid around me
as if i can't face life & never did without him

consider this a letter to prove
i sure as hell

fucking can

Outside in the Streets & Inside in the Safest Room

you say: i'm leaving, leaving, leaving
that should matter, i know, sorry.
a thousand, five hundred & seven days & god knows i can't say it back—

i know it's not wise to smoke indoors, know it leaves ugly yellow stains on the wall
leaves the same stains on my fingers, my lungs, my heart
might as well have my insides match my outsides, or my outsides match my insides...

i say: is it too cold in my house?
you haven't taken your coat off since you entered
but you took your shoes off, you don't plan to march off no matter what—

you say: i'm leaving us, are you listening?
you said once you'd never leave the house
with chipped nail polish & without a brush of mascara...

it's so familiar i can almost feel it now—my hands trembling, my throat closing
you've always said that, expecting it to shatter me
all the ways i've begged & begged for you to stop saying it—

i say: the coat's fashionable, i suppose
never knew what was trendy til now, at least people say so
i'm in a red dress, suppose it's stylish. used to wear black & grey...

i'd wear the same ripped jeans six weeks in a row, my laundry load only
the same three items. i miss those days, when
you could shoebox me as a nightmare & i'd beg you to let me be a dream this time—

i say: sorry, i'm calmer than the pond in your family's backyard
the one before your parents bought a condo in the city
& as you stomp, i think about when we watched that movie with your mom...

& yet, sorry, you hate her, you hate her for...? it's unclear
won't dare to say it's because you crave the attention
i said that a while ago & maybe i'm sorry—

you take off your coat, throw it on the ground
& i realize it was mine—you've been wearing it ever since

i try to remember giving it to you, try to remember the moment it left my heart...

> *you whisper under your breath: how like you to be this way*
> you don't explain what way you mean & i wonder
if i'm being any way at all—or if you're just holding on to a five-year-old expectation—

i pick up my coat, hang it up, close the closet door
> & wonder why you bothered wearing it at all, or today
when you said you hated it so much...

i expect the room to be empty when you leave
expect my heart to match my outsides
& be stained yellow & black

SPRING

Proverbs 16:15
When a king's face brightens, it means life; his favor is like a rain cloud in spring.

Sacred Stones

i go where the world is quiet & all storms go to rest
a warm haven where the coffee is just right—never too hot & never gets cold

there's always a cigarette to be smoked & food to eat
a deck of cards shuffled & dealt & a collection of strange souls to play with

nestled in-between woods & high up in the mountains
where the weather smiles down on me & i'm always properly dressed

there is such a place where my laughter is genuine & all masks are left at the door
all of our planes of existence meet in the middle & never are disrespected

the door jingles a melody when it opens & the windows are vast & the yellow kitchen
rivals the reverence of the sun after days of rain, or rain after a long drought

it doesn't matter that we're weary & bent in strange shapes
our jagged edges blur & blur 'til the noise is filled with blissful silence

there exists such a place with a stone brick wall & wood paneling
& flowers growing all the colors —never grey—

a place i've been living or dying to cultivate
no blueprint, built by intuition & an understanding

that at least i exist here, with
or without you

Wealth Without Knowing

my imaginary friend
haunted me like a ghost
a medium, i created seances
chasing them in the occult

dreaming of their
reflection in my mirror
looking after me

my heartbeat when i blushed
we would visit in dreams
my thrilling action-adventures

no matter what the night brought
they guided me around every bullet

4ams spent in a sweat
to feel them & see them
a feeling you get in horror movies
hallways that seem to stretch on and on

every road possible, i took
& lost parts of myself to false echoes
nothing more than noise

spent my life waiting
for this richness
i already had

for we did not meet
by accident

To The Glory

pause / rewind / start again
mind clearing / going blank

emptiness that deletes / destroys
wander / sit / wander again

a slow fade into warmth
erase hollow thoughts

where flowers bloom & the world quiets
& i sing:

i am dead / i am awake
i am i am i am

the empty sky & a glimpse of day
in a very long something else

swimming in bliss / watching my splendor come
synchronicity of things aligning

somehow the sun manages
to set from all sides

the water ebbs, the breeze blows
surrounded by

a golden halo

The Power of The Tongue

& so once more the words get stuck on my tongue
sweet sweet honey / crystals unlike broken glass
sugar caked on my lips i keep these words to myself

wait & see where this road will lead
unexpected journey & trailing the lines of your body
& learning to thrive when love is not enough

when the stars are crossed & the sun won't come out
& a new pain learned when you're left alone
messages never sent & never read

you cauterize the wound by writing &
wrap the pain in a yellow ribbon
& send it away to be felt by someone else

love does not possess & it does not hold tally
of mistakes & missteps
i carry those bruises

but i still love
i still
love

Miloh Gorgevska lives in the dreary suburbs outside of Toronto, Ontario. Nonbinary and queer, they identify as a menace to society's traditions. As a jack-of-all-trades, they are an author, director, poet & screenwriter. Writing has been their purpose for the majority of their life.

Previously, their writing under the pen name 'Kara Petrovic' has been published in Philadelphia Stories, Train: A Poetry Journal & others. Their poetry collections are available for purchase at most major sellers.

SHARDS, their debut short film, was awarded Best Cinematography and placed at festivals worldwide. As well as writing and directing 3 other, smaller short films, they have been nominated twice for Best Script at IFFNY & PAMA in 2022. Prior to that, they had been an actor for 8 years, appearing in short films and a CBCKids show.

A graduate of Toronto Metropolitan University, they have a particular focus on telling true stories that are taboo and uncomfortably emotional.

Twitter: @bye_mielo
Instagram: @miegorge
TikTok: @bye_mielo

Also Available from Cathexis Northwest Press:

<u>Something To Cry About</u>
by Robert Krantz

<u>Suburban Hermeneutics</u>
by Ian Cappelli

<u>God's Love Is Very Busy</u>
by David Seung

<u>that one time we were almost people</u>
by Christian Czaniecki

<u>Fever Dream/Take Heart</u>
by Valyntina Grenier

<u>The Book of Night & Waking</u>
by Clif Mason

<u>Dead Birds of New Zealand</u>
by Christian Czaniecki

<u>The Weathering of Igneous Rockforms in High-Altitude Riparian Environments</u>
by John Belk

<u>If A Fish</u>
by George Burns

<u>How to Draw a Blank</u>
by Collin Van Son

<u>En Route</u>
by Jesse Wolfe

<u>sky bright psalms</u>
by Temple Cone

<u>Moonbird</u>
by Henry G. Stanton

<u>southern athiest. oh, honey</u>
by d. e. fulford

<u>Bruises, Birthmarks & Other Calamities</u>
by Nadine Klassen

<u>Wanted: Comedy, Addicts</u>
by AR Dugan

<u>They Curve Like Snakes</u>
by David Alexander McFarland

<u>the catalog of daily fears</u>
by Beth Dufford

<u>Shops Close Too Early</u>
by Josh Feit

<u>Vanity Unfair and Other Poems</u>
by Robert Eugene Rubino

<u>Bodies of Separation</u>
by Chim Sher Ting

Cathexis Northwest Press

www.ingramcontent.com/pod-product-compliance
Lightning Source LLC
Chambersburg PA
CBHW030351100526
44592CB00010B/919